Saxon
INVADERS
AND SETTLERS

Tony D. Triggs

Wayland

Invaders and Settlers

Norman Invaders and Settlers

Roman Invaders and Settlers

Saxon Invaders and Settlers

Viking Invaders and Settlers

Series Editor: James Kerr

Designer: Loraine Hayes

Consultant: Mark Gardiner BA FSA MIFA Deputy Director, Field Archaeology Unit (Institute of Archaeology, London).

This edition published in 1994 by Wayland (Publishers) Limited

First published in 1992 by Wayland (Publishers) Limited, 61 Western Road, Hove, East Sussex, BN3 1JD

© Copyright 1992 Wayland (Publishers) Limited

British Library Cataloguing in Publication Data
Triggs, Tony D.
   Saxon invaders and settlers.—(Invaders and settlers)
   I. Title II. Series
   942.01

HARDBACK ISBN 0-7502-0534-2

PAPERBACK ISBN 0-7502-1356-6

Typeset by Dorchester Typesetting Group Limited
Printed and bound in Italy by Rotolito Lombarda S.p.A., Milan

Opposite:

Top:	Coins found at Sutton Hoo, East Anglia.
Middle:	Lindisfarne Priory, built on the site of a Saxon monastery.
Bottom:	Reconstruction of King Redwald's helmet.

Cover:

Extreme top:	Coin found at Sutton Hoo, East Anglia.
Top left:	A burial urn.
Top middle:	A rebuilt Saxon hut at West Stow, Suffolk.
Top right:	The Alfred Jewel.
Bottom left:	A page from the *Anglo-Saxon Chronicle*.
Bottom middle:	King Redwald's helmet.
Bottom right:	Anglo-Saxon settlements in Britain.
Back:	A brooch found at West Stow.

CONTENTS

All words that appear in **bold** in the text are defined in the glossary.

The Saxons arrive

Part of Hadrian's Wall, which the Romans built across northern England.

Two thousand years ago, the people who lived in England, Wales and parts of southern Scotland were called Britons. They kept sheep on the hills and made themselves clothes from the sheep's wool. They grew wheat, peas and other crops in the valleys. They lived in large family groups on farms, and their homes were circular wooden huts.

In AD 43, Roman soldiers from Europe conquered England and Wales. They used stone to build towns and country villas. They also built **forts** and camps for their soldiers, and straight roads for the soldiers to use.

People called Saxons, who came from Germany, sometimes rowed across the North Sea and raided the coast of south-east England. They probably wanted to

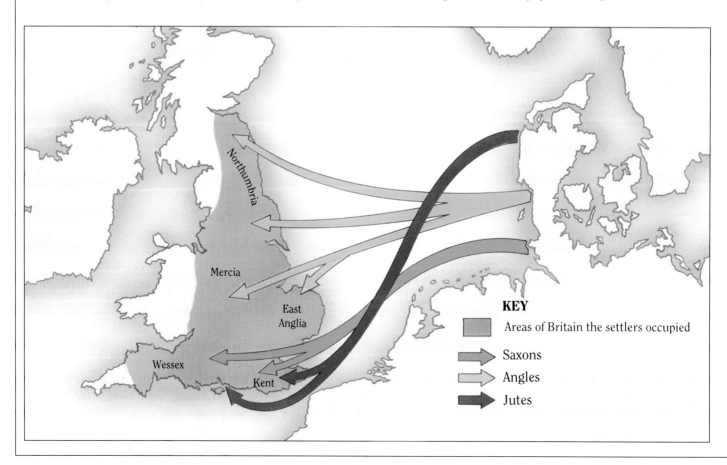

Northumbria

Mercia

East Anglia

Wessex

Kent

KEY

Areas of Britain the settlers occupied

Saxons

Angles

Jutes

The Romans built this fort at Portchester on the south coast of England.

settle in England, but the Romans always drove them away. Then in AD 410 the Romans left Britain and returned to Europe. They told the Britons that they would have to defend themselves against Saxon raids.

We know about some of these things from a book called the *Anglo-Saxon Chronicle*. The book is like a diary because Saxons added new things by hand every year. The *Chronicle* mentions a British king called Vortigern, and it says that in AD 449:

*. . . he gave some Saxons land in south-east England in exchange for their help in fighting the **Picts**. They fought the Picts and had victory in all their battles. The Saxons then sent to Germany for more men, saying that the Britons did not have the strength to defend their own rich lands.*

The old man in this picture is passing on his land to his eldest son. The younger sons will have to sail to another country to get land.

The Saxons soon sent many men to help the others. There were Angles and Jutes as well as Saxons. They were led by two brothers, Hengest and Horsa. They first dealt with Vortigern's enemies; then they turned on the King and the Britons, using fire and swords to defeat them.

The *Chronicle* says that the Angles, Saxons and Jutes divided England up between them. Each area had a different king. Nowadays we use the word 'Saxon' to refer to all three tribes.

No one is sure why the Saxons came. Some people think that Saxon fathers always left their land to their eldest sons, forcing younger sons to find new land in other countries. It is also hard to be sure how the Saxons treated the Britons. They probably turned some of them into slaves.

The Saxons did not like the Romans' cities. They said that they were 'the work of giants' and let the buildings fall into ruins.

A Saxon village

The Saxons lived in small groups of huts in villages. Most of the villages have grown into modern villages or towns, and things the Saxons left in the soil are buried under modern buildings.

In a few places, the Saxons left their villages and no one lived there again. The buildings fell down and disappeared, but clues in the soil tell us about the Saxons' lives. West Stow in Suffolk is one of the best examples of this. The Saxons built a village there as soon as they arrived in England. They lived in the village for 200 years then moved to another site nearby. Well over 1,000 years went by until, in the twentieth century, some **archaeologists** noticed that rabbits were digging up pieces of Saxon pottery. The archaeologists removed the grass and the surface soil, and they started to find broken combs, lumps of clay and some little patches of darkened soil. The patches showed where the wooden posts of Saxon buildings had rotted away.

Holes in the soil where the posts of a Saxon hall once stood.

The huts in a Saxon village were usually built in groups. Each group belonged to one large family, including relatives such as uncles and aunts. There was often a larger building, or hall, at the centre of each group of huts. The family met in the hall and worked and slept in the huts. In West Stow there were four or five families and each family probably had some slaves.

One of the rebuilt houses at West Stow.

Making a Saxon hut

You need some long, thin pieces of wood and a shoe box or a similar carton. (Save the lid as you may need the cardboard later.)

1 Cut a doorway in one side of the box, and place the box on a tray of sand or soil.

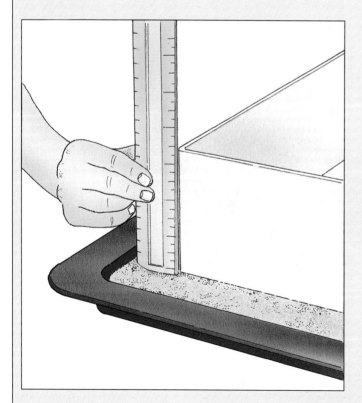

2 Measure the box to see how tall it is.

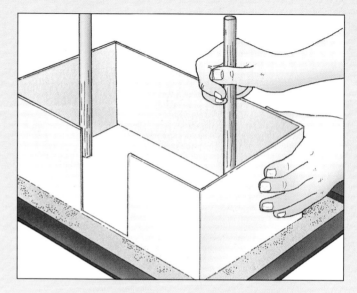

3 Take two lengths of wood about two and a half times as tall as the box. Push them through the bottom of the box quite near to each end. They should stand upright in the sand, with the tops twice as high as the sides of the box.

4 Take a third length of wood. This should be as long as the box and you should glue it to the tops of the upright lengths.

Rebuilding a Saxon house at West Stow.

6 Use card to fill the triangular space at each end of the hut, then paint or cover the walls so that they look as if they are made of wooden planks.

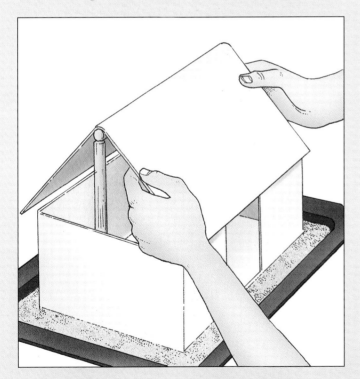

5 Make a sloping roof with card or straw. Straw is best because the Saxons used thatch.

7 Put a flat piece of plasticine or clay with some sticks on it in the hut to look like a fire. Add a model family.

Clothes worn by a typical Saxon family for work in the fields.

On the site of some Saxon huts, archaeologists have found rings of clay from the villagers' weaving **looms**. The villagers tied woollen threads along the top of their looms. They weighted the threads with rings of clay to keep them taut. Then they wove other threads from side to side to make cloth.

Archaeologists think Saxon looms were like this.

Saxon villagers kept lots of sheep, and archaeologists sometimes find the shears the Saxons used for removing the wool. They also find bones from sheep, hens, geese, goats, cattle and pigs. The Saxons kept these animals in and around their villages. When archaeologists find odd bones, they know that the animal was killed, cut up and eaten. But the Saxons kept animals for milk, butter, cheese and eggs, as well as meat. They also kept oxen to pull their ploughs.

The villagers made their own clay pots for cooking and storing food, and for keeping the water they got from streams. They had to dig up the clay themselves; then they rolled it into 'snakes' and coiled them up to make the pots. The villagers baked the pots in a bonfire to make them hard.

Loom weights and needles from West Stow.

The scene inside a Saxon hall. (The houses were smaller.)

Making a Saxon pot

You will need some sort of modelling clay, such as plasticine.

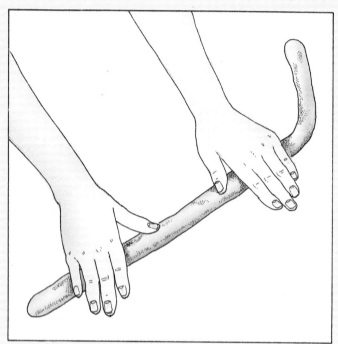

1 Roll the clay under your hands to make a long 'snake'.

3 Roll some more snakes and build up the sides of your pot.

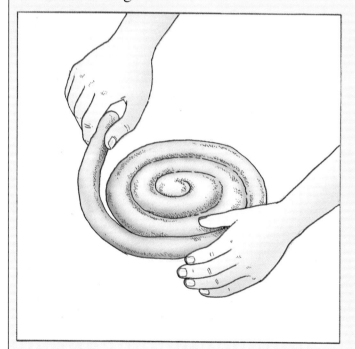

2 Coil the 'snake' round and round to make a base for your pot.

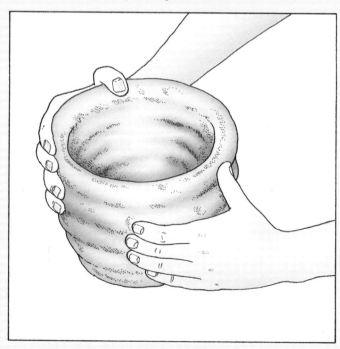

4 When your pot is complete try to make the sides smoother and close any cracks.

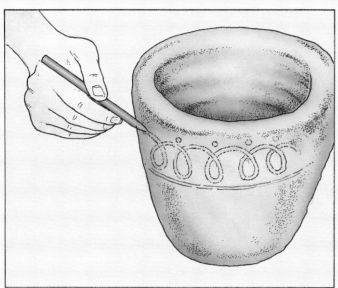

5   The Saxons sometimes put patterns on their pots. Try to put similar patterns on yours.

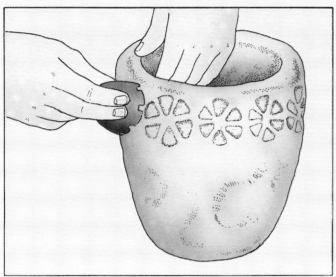

6   The Saxons sometimes took a piece of bone or antler and made a simple shape on the end, then they pressed it into the soft clay all round the pot. If you want to copy this method you will have to choose something you can cut easily and safely. If your clay is soft enough you could try using a piece of potato. Or make your pattern with something which already has an interesting shape.

Saxon villagers made this pot for mead or wine.

The Saxons' pots sometimes give us clues about the crops they grew. Seeds got into the clay. When the pots were baked, the seeds were burned, but they left little holes in the side of the pots; the shape of the holes shows what sort of seeds they were. At West Stow, grains of wheat got mixed up in the clay. Archaeologists have also found a single pea in the soil. So the villagers may have eaten peas. A nearby village called Peasenhall got its name from all the peas it grew.

Archaeologists have found cheap **bronze** brooches at the sites of many Saxon villages. Sometimes brooches from neighbouring villages are just the same. There must have been traders who made brooches and rode round selling them to women in each village in their area. Perhaps the villagers paid the traders by giving them cloth to sell to people who could not make enough. Some Saxon villages produced such a lot of cloth that merchants were able to sell it abroad.

When they came to England, the Saxons were pagans. Pagans are people who believe in many gods. The Saxons probably believed that the dead would need their property in another life. The people at West Stow buried their dead near the village, putting their favourite possessions beside them in their graves.

This woman's brooch was found at West Stow, and similar ones were found in nearby villages.

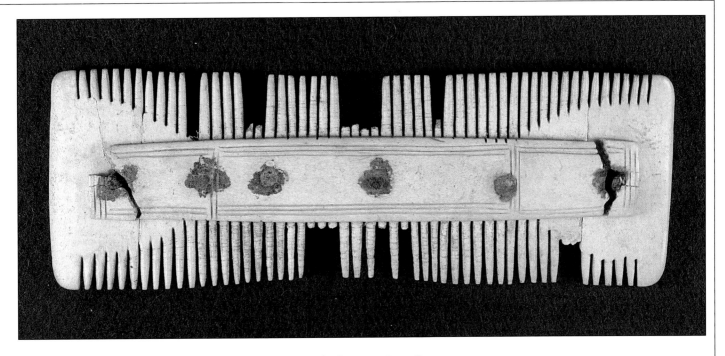

A comb from West Stow.

Sometimes the Saxons burned their dead to ashes and put the ashes in pots to be buried, perhaps with something small like a comb.

Grave goods give us clues about the different jobs men and women did. Women's graves often contain sewing boxes; men's graves often contain knives and spears. This suggests that women did the spinning, weaving and sewing while men did the hunting, fighting and farming. Sometimes women's graves have sets of keys. They were specially made as a sign that women looked after the family's goods and ran the home.

This pot was made for someone's ashes. The person's name was written on it in letters called runes.

17

A royal graveyard

The King of East Anglia lived at a place called Rendlesham. The River Deben ran near to his wooden palace, and visitors who had crossed the North Sea could row up the river in less than an hour. The river ran past a hill which seemed to guard the way to Rendlesham. At the top of the hill was the royal graveyard.

In AD 625, the King, whose name was Redwald, died. Redwald was not just the King of East Anglia; he was also the *bretwalda* (the most important king in England). Because he was so important, he had a very solemn funeral. Forty of Redwald's servants rowed a boat to the foot of the hill, then they hauled it to the top and lowered it into a huge grave. Redwald's family and other servants carried his body from Rendlesham, and they placed it in the middle of the ship with jewellery, weapons and other goods.

Sometimes servants were killed and buried in their owners' graves; perhaps the Saxons thought that a buried servant would go on working for his or her master or mistress in the land of the dead.

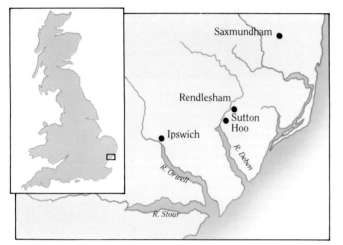

ABOVE *Redwald had two of these clasps to do up his cloak at the shoulders.*
RIGHT *Burying Redwald's ship.*

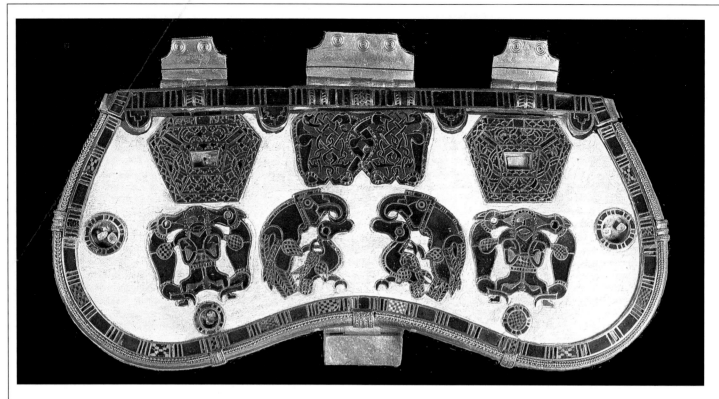

This is the lid of King Redwald's purse. It was full of coins, including the ones you can see opposite.

This helmet was made to show what Redwald's helmet was like before it was buried.

We cannot be certain that any of Redwald's servants were killed, but people were strangled and buried nearby without any grave goods. Perhaps they had no goods because they were very poor, and this suggests that they were slaves.

Some of Redwald's slaves built a huge mound of soil over his grave. There were other mounds in the graveyard, but Redwald's mound was the biggest of all.

Fifty years later, the royal family left their wooden palace, which rotted away and disappeared. People forgot what the mounds were for, although some people said there was treasure inside them. Almost 1,000 years later, in the time of Queen Elizabeth I and William Shakespeare, a gang of robbers opened the mounds and took all they could find.

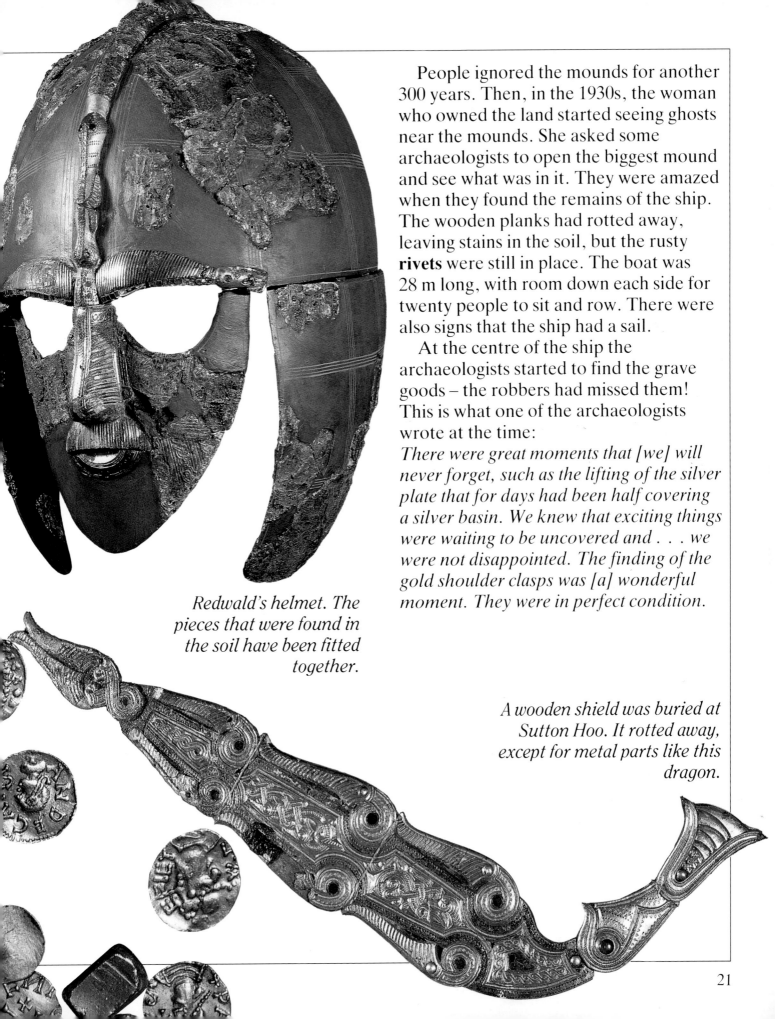

People ignored the mounds for another 300 years. Then, in the 1930s, the woman who owned the land started seeing ghosts near the mounds. She asked some archaeologists to open the biggest mound and see what was in it. They were amazed when they found the remains of the ship. The wooden planks had rotted away, leaving stains in the soil, but the rusty **rivets** were still in place. The boat was 28 m long, with room down each side for twenty people to sit and row. There were also signs that the ship had a sail.

At the centre of the ship the archaeologists started to find the grave goods – the robbers had missed them! This is what one of the archaeologists wrote at the time:

There were great moments that [we] will never forget, such as the lifting of the silver plate that for days had been half covering a silver basin. We knew that exciting things were waiting to be uncovered and . . . we were not disappointed. The finding of the gold shoulder clasps was [a] wonderful moment. They were in perfect condition.

Redwald's helmet. The pieces that were found in the soil have been fitted together.

A wooden shield was buried at Sutton Hoo. It rotted away, except for metal parts like this dragon.

The Saxons become Christians

The Saxons built this beautiful church at Bradford-on-Avon near Bristol.

During Redwald's lifetime, a band of Christian **missionaries** from Rome had landed in Kent. Led by a man called Augustine, they persuaded the King of Kent to become a Christian, and some of them travelled to Northumbria and **preached** to the King and people there.

The Saxons had not conquered Wales or Ireland. The people living there were already Christians. Some Irish monks built a **monastery** on Lindisfarne, an island off the Northumbrian coast, and they too taught the Saxons Christianity.

Once they became Christians, the Saxons put up stone crosses with Christian words and pictures carved on them. They gathered round the crosses to pray. Later, they built proper churches.

Few Saxons settled in central or northern Scotland, but southern Scotland was part of Northumbria. The Saxons at Ruthwell, near Dumfries, built a beautiful cross that can still be seen. The cross is decorated with pictures, and there is part of a poem about a cross. It is carved in mysterious letters called runes.

LEFT *The Ruthwell Cross, which used to stand in the open air.*

RIGHT *A model of the monastery at Jarrow where the monk Bede lived and worked.*

This grandstand stood near a palace at Yeavering in Northumbria.
People probably used it to listen to Christian preachers.

ᚠ = æ	= a	= b	ᚳ = c	= d	= e	= f	= g	= h	= i
ᛄ = j	ᚲ = k	= l	= m	= n	ᚸ = ng	= o	ᚹ = p	ᚹþ = qu	= r
= s	ᛏ = t	þ = th	ᚢ = u	ᚡ = v	= w	ᚤ = x	ᚨ = y	ᛉ = z	

Two sorts of writing

The Saxons had two ways of writing things. They used ordinary letters and they also used runes. Here is a Saxon sentence written in both ways:

ᚻᛁᛋ ᛏᚨᛗᚨ ᚹᚨᛋ ᚱᛖᛞᚹᚨᛚᛞ ᚨᛏᛞ ᚻᛁᛋ ᚹᛁᚠᛖᛋ ᛏᚨᛗᚨ ᚹᚨᛋ ᛖᚦᛖᛚᛒᛖᚱᚷᚨ

His nama wæs Redwald ond his wifes nama wæs Ethelberga

Things to do

1 Write down what you think the sentence means.
2 Copy out the table above and fill in all the missing runes. (You will need to study the Saxon sentence carefully.)
3 Write your name in runes, or use them to send a secret message to a friend.

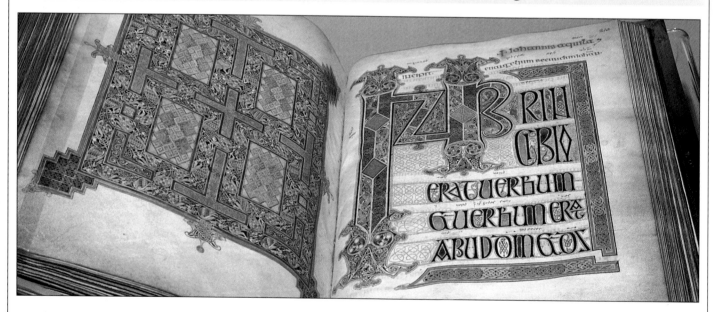

Pages from the Lindisfarne Gospels. As Christians, the Saxons thought the Gospels were holy, so they made these copies as beautiful as possible. For paper they used animals' skins, which they beat until they were smooth and soft.

The Vikings attack

The year AD 793 was a very unpleasant time for the Saxons. According to the *Chronicle:*

. . . fierce and threatening signs came over the land of Northumbria, and terrified the people. There were severe whirlwinds and thunderstorms, and fiery dragons flying in the sky. Crops failed, people went hungry, and shortly afterwards **heathen** *men destroyed God's church on Lindisfarne with robbery and brutal murder.*

The 'heathen men' were Vikings. They were very skilful sailors indeed, and they came from Norway, Sweden and Denmark (the Vikings from Denmark are sometimes called Danes). For the next 250 years they raided all the coasts they could reach. They sailed across the Atlantic Ocean, settling in Iceland and Greenland and visiting North America. They also settled in Ireland, northern France and other parts of Europe.

The Vikings made a fresh attack on England in AD 835. After that they came nearly every summer. They stole what they could and escaped in their boats. Then in AD 855 they spent the winter on an island off the coast of Kent. The Saxons kept sheep there and they called it Sheep Island.

The water all round the island stopped the sheep from straying, but it also stopped the Saxons from getting rid of the Vikings. To make matters worse, the

The Normans built this priory on the site of the Saxon monastery at Lindisfarne.

Vikings were eating the Saxons' sheep, and were probably planning to stay for good.

All round the coasts of England and Scotland the Vikings began to take land and build villages. Danish armies marched across England, frightening people and taking their money. Sometimes the Saxons paid the Danes to leave them alone; but in the end they usually took the Saxons' land as well as their money.

This is called the Alfred Jewel because the letters round the edge say Ælfred mec heht gewyrcan – King Alfred had me made. It had a pointer at the end and was probably used in a church for keeping the place in a holy book.

In the middle of winter in AD 878, the Danes attacked King Alfred of Wessex. The Saxons used to have midwinter feasts, and Alfred's house at Chippenham in Wiltshire was probably full of laughter and mead (one of the Saxons' favourite drinks). We cannot be sure how the Danes attacked; perhaps they set the building on fire.

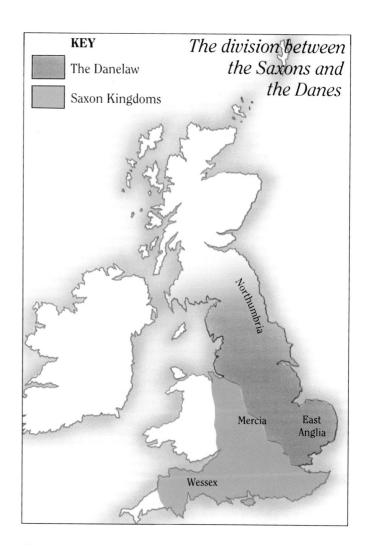

A page from the Chronicle.

According to the *Chronicle:*
Alfred and a few of his men escaped through the woods . . . and built a fort at Athelney in Somerset. Then, in the seventh week after Easter, he rode to Egbert's Stone, east of Selwood. The fighting men of Somerset, Wiltshire and part of Hampshire met him there – they were overjoyed that he had come. The next day they left their camp and went to . . . Edington, where they fought with the whole Danish force and made them run away. They chased them to their fortress and surrounded them for fourteen days and fourteen nights. Then the Danes gave Alfred **hostages**, *and they swore that they would leave his kingdom.*

Alfred encouraged the Danish king to become a Christian. Then the two rulers agreed that the Danes would have eastern England, but Saxon kings would still rule Wessex and part of Mercia. The Danes' part of England was known as the Danelaw.

KEY

The Danelaw

Saxon Kingdoms

The division between the Saxons and the Danes

Northumbria

Mercia

East Anglia

Wessex

Saxon towns

Under the Saxons, towns grew up in various ways. Some began as fortresses. Alfred wanted to make sure the Danes stayed out of Wessex and the Saxon part of Mercia, so he chose some villages just outside the Danelaw and made the Saxons build walls round them. The walls were usually made of earth, with a sturdy fence on top. The villagers were ready to fight off the Danes if they tried to attack. Other local people could go to the fortress for safety or to join in the fighting.

Alfred's son and daughter had other fortresses built in many parts of Wessex and Mercia. The villages in the fortresses quickly grew into towns. This was because Saxon kings encouraged people to live there so that there would always be plenty of men to defend the fortresses. Wallingford in Berkshire was one of King Alfred's fortified towns, and we can still see where the walls used to run. The fortress guarded a **ford** across the River Thames. The town had walls round three sides and the river ran along the fourth side.

The town of Wallingford, seen from the air. The arrow marks one corner of the Saxon wall. See if you can trace other parts of it.

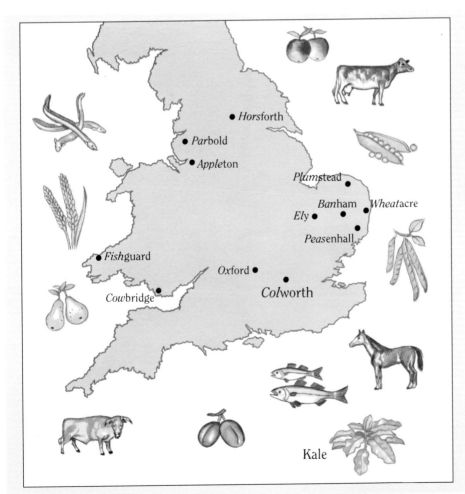

Clues in names

Most places in Britain got their names in Saxon times. Some of the names tell us what sort of crop or animal the Saxons grew or kept in the place. For example, Appleton was a place where the Saxons grew lots of apples.

Look at the place-names on the map and try to match them up with the drawings. Then make a list of places and crops or animals. Put one pair of words on each line. You could start with:

Colworth – kale.

You can do the rest in any order.

The Norman Conquest

The Vikings and the Saxons in the Danelaw usually lived in peace, but there were wars between Viking and Saxon kings. They fought to control the whole of England. A Saxon king called Harold ruled England in AD 1066, but in that year the Vikings in northern France sent an army against him. We call the Vikings from northern France Normans; this is short for Northmen, or Men from the North. The story of how they conquered England is told in the Bayeux Tapestry. The Tapestry is like a huge comic strip, and the pictures were done with needle and thread. Saxon women made the Tapestry, and it shows how skilful they were at **embroidery**.

The Saxons were good at other things too. They made up all sorts of riddles and poems, and people still enjoy their exciting poem called *Beowulf*. The hero Beowulf kills two monsters; later he fights a dragon that guards an enormous treasure. They kill each other, and Beowulf's followers take the treasure and bury it in Beowulf's tomb.

This picture from the Bayeux Tapestry shows the Norman army sailing to England.

Beowulf fights the dragon.

Museums have treasure from real Saxon graves, and they also have things that tell us about the Saxons' lives. At West Stow in Suffolk, archaeologists have rebuilt a Saxon village, and Saxon churches can be seen all over England. Many other things, such as hedges, fields, roads and towns, are on sites the Saxons chose 1,000 years ago. Signs of their work are all around us!

AD 400	The Romans leave Britain. The Britons ask the Saxons to help them fight the Picts. More and more Saxons settle in England and southern Scotland.
AD 500	The Saxons fight and defeat the Britons.
AD 600	Missionaries arrive from Rome. Redwald is buried at Sutton Hoo.
AD 700	Carved cross put up at Ruthwell (Dumfriesshire). King Offa rules Mercia.
AD 800	The Danes begin raiding. They destroy many churches and monasteries. The Danes start to settle in England, but Alfred saves Wessex and part of Mercia.
AD 900	Alfred's son Athelstan becomes King of England.
AD 1000	King Ethelred loses England to the Danes. England returns to Saxon rule. The Battle of Hastings – Norman kings come to power in England.
AD 1100	

Glossary

Archaeologist   Someone who digs up and studies objects and remains from the past.

Bronze   A mixture of the metals copper and tin.

Embroidery   Patterns or pictures stitched on to cloth.

Ford   A shallow area in a river that can be crossed on foot or horseback.

Fort, Fortress   A sort of castle; sometimes just an area with walls or ditches to keep out attackers.

Grave goods   Belongings that are put in someone's grave.

Heathens   People who believe in many gods.

Hostages   Prisoners who are captured and held so that they can be used to bargain with the enemy.

Loom   A sort of frame on which people weave cloth.

Missionaries   People who travel to another country and try to persuade the people there to change their religion.

Monastery   A place where people live, pray and obey strict rules because of what they believe about God.

Picts   One of the warlike tribes of Scotland.

Preach   To persuade people about religious ideas.

Rivets   Things like bolts used for joining planks together.

Books to read

The Anglo-Saxon Chronicles edited and translated by A Savage (Papermac, 1984)

Anglo-Saxon England by L and J Laing (Granada, 1982)

Dark Age Britain: What to See and Where by R Jackson (P Stephens, 1984)

Growing Up in the Dark Ages by B Ralph Lewis (Batsford, 1980)

A Guide to Anglo-Saxon Sites by N and M Kerr (Granada, 1982)

Saxon Britain by T D Triggs (Wayland, 1989)

Saxon Villages by R Place (Wayland, 1989)

The Saxons by T D Triggs (Oliver & Boyd, 1982)

Places to visit

Churches, monasteries and cemeteries
Bradford-on-Avon, Wiltshire
Bradwell-on-Sea, Essex
Brixworth, Northamptonshire
Canterbury, Kent
Conisborough, South Yorkshire
Earls Barton, Northamptonshire
Escomb, County Durham
Iona, Strathclyde
Ledsham, West Yorkshire
Lindisfarne, Northumberland
North Elmham, Norfolk

Crosses
Bewcastle, Cumbria
Ilkley, West Yorkshire
Middleton, North Yorkshire
Ruthwell, Dumfriesshire
St Andrews, Fife
Whitby, North Yorkshire

Earthworks
Offa's Dyke, which is best seen north of
    Knighton, Powys

Reconstructed Saxon huts
West Stow, near Bury St Edmunds,
    Suffolk

Town defences
Wallingford, Oxfordshire
Wareham, Dorset

Museums
Ashmolean Museum, Oxford
Bede Monastery Museum, Jarrow
British Museum, London
Dumfries Museum, Dumfriesshire
Hull City Museum, Hull
Moyses Hall Museum, Bury St Edmunds
Museum of London, London
National Museum of Antiquities of
    Scotland, Edinburgh
Norwich Castle Museum, Norwich
Sheffield City Museum, Sheffield
University Museum of Archaeology and
    Anthropology, Cambridge
Yorkshire Museum, York

Illuminated manuscripts
Durham Cathedral
Lichfield Cathedral

Picture Acknowledgements

The publisher would like to thank the following for
providing the pictures used in this book: Ancient Art and
Architecture Collection cover (top right), 22 (bottom
left), 24 (bottom), 25 (bottom), 30; © Crown copyright
1992 MoD. Reproduced with the permission of the
Controller of HMSO 27 (top); C M Dixon cover (top and
top left), title page, contents page (bottom and middle), 4
(top), 5, 17 (bottom), 18, 20 (bottom), 21 (bottom), 25,
31; E T Archives Limited cover (bottom left), 26; Michael
Holford cover (bottom middle), 15, 20 (top), 21 (top and
middle), 22 (top), 28; St Paul's Jarrow Development Trust
23 (bottom right); West Stow Anglo-Saxon Village Trust
cover (top middle), back cover, contents page (top), 7, 9,
11, 12, 13 (top and bottom), 16, 17 (top).

Artwork: Peter Bull 4, 10-11, 14-15, 18, 24, 26, 27, 29
(right); Peter Dennis 6, 8, 12, 19, 23; R. Mooney 29 (left);
Malcolm S Walker cover (bottom right).

Index

The numbers in **bold** refer to captions.